Table Of Contents

Introduction

Explanation of the book's purpose

The purpose of this book, "No Code, No Problem: Creating Business Apps Without Coding Skills," is to provide business owners with the knowledge and tools they need to create custom apps for their businesses without having to rely on a team of developers or learn how to code themselves.

In today's digital age, having a business app can be a game-changer. It can help you connect with your customers, streamline your operations, and ultimately grow your business. However, the process of creating an app can be daunting, especially if you don't have any coding skills.

That's where the concept of "no code" comes in. No code platforms allow you to create custom apps using visual interfaces and drag-and-drop tools, without ever having to write a single line of code. This means that anyone, regardless of their technical background, can create a professional-looking app for their business.

The purpose of this book is to guide you through the process of creating a business app using a no code platform. We'll start by exploring the benefits of having a business app, and then dive into the world of no code. We'll introduce you to popular no code platforms and help you choose the one that's right for your business.

From there, we'll walk you through the process of designing and building your app, step-by-step. We'll cover everything from creating a user interface to integrating with other software and services. We'll also provide tips and tricks to help you make your app stand out in a crowded marketplace.

Throughout the book, we'll use real-world examples to illustrate how businesses of all sizes and niches are using no code platforms to create custom apps. We'll also provide exercises and quizzes to help you test your knowledge and make sure you're on the right track.

By the end of this book, you'll have the skills and confidence you need to create a custom app for your business using a no code platform. Whether you want to create an app to connect with your customers, streamline your operations, or something else entirely, this book will help you make it happen.

Who should read the book

Who Should Read the Book?

If you are a business owner who has always wanted to create a mobile application for your business but lacks the technical skills to do so, this book is for you. No Code, No Problem: Creating Business Apps Without Coding Skills is the ultimate guide to help you design, develop, and launch your business app without writing a single line of code.

This book is not just for business owners who want to create an app. It is also for anyone who wants to learn how to build a mobile application without coding skills. If you are an entrepreneur, marketer, or student who wants to learn how to make an app for your business, this book is a must-read.

How To Make an App for My Business

Many business owners have the misconception that they need to hire expensive developers or learn coding skills to create a mobile application for their business. However, with the rise of no-code platforms, anyone can build a mobile app without any coding experience.

In this book, you will learn how to use no-code platforms to create a business app that meets your specific needs. You will learn how to design the user interface, add functionalities, and launch your app on app stores without any coding skills.

Moreover, this book is divided into easy-to-follow chapters that cover every aspect of creating a mobile application without coding. You will learn how to choose the right no-code platform, create wireframes, design prototypes, and test your app before launching it.

Conclusion

In conclusion, No Code, No Problem: Creating Business Apps Without Coding Skills is an essential guide for business owners who want to create a mobile application without coding skills. This book is also suitable for anyone who wants to learn how to make an app for their business. With this book, you will learn how to design, develop, and launch your business app without writing a single line of code. Get your copy today and start building your business app!

Benefits of learning how to create business apps without coding skills

As a business owner, you may feel overwhelmed by the prospect of creating an app for your business. You may think that you need to have coding skills or hire a developer to make an app. However, with the rise of no-code app development platforms, you can create a professional-looking app without any coding knowledge. In this subchapter, we will explore the benefits of learning how to create business apps without coding skills.

1. Saves time and money

Learning how to create business apps without coding skills can save you time and money. Hiring a developer to create an app can be expensive and time-consuming. With no-code app development platforms, you can create an app in a fraction of the time and at a lower cost.

2. Easy to use

No-code app development platforms are designed for non-technical users. You don't need to have any coding skills to create an app. The platforms provide drag-and-drop tools that make it easy to create an app without any technical knowledge.

3. Customizable

No-code app development platforms allow you to customize your app to meet your business needs. You can choose from a range of templates and features to create an app that reflects your brand and meets your business goals.

4. Increases customer engagement

Having an app for your business can increase customer engagement. Your app can provide customers with easy access to your products and services, and allow them to interact with your brand through features such as push notifications and loyalty programs.

5. Improves business efficiency

An app can improve business efficiency by streamlining processes and reducing manual tasks. For example, you can create an app that allows customers to book appointments or order products directly from their mobile device, reducing the need for manual processes.

In conclusion, learning how to create business apps without coding skills can be a game-changer for your business. It can save you time and money, improve customer engagement, and increase business efficiency. With no-code app development platforms, you can create a professional-looking app that meets your business needs without any coding knowledge.

Explanation of the no-code movement

The no-code movement is a revolutionary concept in the world of technology that has opened up a whole new world of opportunities for business owners who want to create their own apps without having to learn coding skills. The idea behind the no-code movement is to provide business owners with a platform that enables them to create their own mobile apps, web apps, and other software applications without the need for any coding experience.

The no-code movement is based on the premise that businesses need to be agile, flexible, and innovative to stay ahead in the competitive landscape. By providing business owners with a no-code development platform, they can easily create and iterate on their own apps, without having to rely on expensive developers or IT departments.

One of the key benefits of the no-code movement is that it allows business owners to take control of their app development process. They no longer have to rely on third-party developers who may not fully understand their business needs or may not be able to deliver the app on time or on budget. With a no-code platform, business owners can create their own apps that are tailored to their specific business needs, which can help improve productivity, streamline processes, and enhance the overall customer experience.

Another benefit of the no-code movement is that it helps to democratize technology. By removing the need for coding skills, anyone can create an app, regardless of their technical background. This opens up opportunities for small business owners, entrepreneurs, and even non-profits to create their own apps, which can help to level the playing field in the business world.

Overall, the no-code movement is a game-changer for business owners who want to create their own apps without having to learn coding skills. It provides a platform that is easy to use, affordable, and flexible, which can help businesses to stay ahead of the curve and innovate in today's fast-paced business environment.

Understanding No Code

Explanation of no-code tools

The world of technology is constantly evolving, and it has become increasingly important for businesses to keep up with the latest trends and tools to stay ahead of the competition. One of the latest trends in the world of tech is the emergence of no-code tools, which have revolutionized the way businesses create apps for their operations.

No-code tools are essentially software platforms that allow users to create applications without the need for coding skills. These tools offer a range of benefits for businesses, including reduced costs, increased efficiency, and improved flexibility.

One of the key advantages of no-code tools is that they eliminate the need for businesses to hire expensive developers to create their apps. With no-code tools, business owners can create their own apps using simple drag-and-drop interfaces and pre-built templates. This not only saves money but also allows businesses to create apps quickly and efficiently.

Another advantage of no-code tools is that they offer a high level of flexibility. Business owners can easily make changes to their apps as needed, without having to wait for a developer to make the changes for them. This allows businesses to be more responsive to changes in their operations and to adapt quickly to new trends in the market.

No-code tools also offer a range of features that can help businesses automate their operations and improve efficiency. For example, many no-code tools offer integrations with popular business software platforms, such as Salesforce and Zapier, allowing businesses to automate tasks and workflows.

Overall, no-code tools offer a range of benefits for businesses looking to create apps for their operations. They are affordable, flexible, and easy to use, making them an ideal solution for businesses of all sizes and industries. Whether you are looking to create a simple app for your business or a more complex system, no-code tools can help you achieve your goals quickly and efficiently.

Advantages of using no-code tools

Advantages of Using No-Code Tools

As a business owner, your focus is on growing your business and making it successful. However, one of the biggest challenges you face is creating and managing different business applications. This is where no-code tools come in handy. No-code tools make it possible to create business applications without having to write a single line of code. Here are some of the advantages of using no-code tools for your business applications.

1. Faster Development

One of the biggest advantages of using no-code tools is the speed of development. Traditional app development can take months or even years to complete. With no-code tools, you can create a fully functional app in days or even hours. This means you can get your app to market faster, giving you a competitive advantage.

2. Cost-Effective

No-code tools are also cost-effective. Traditional app development can be quite expensive, especially if you have to hire a team of developers. With no-code tools, you can create your app yourself, saving you a lot of money. This is particularly beneficial for small businesses with limited budgets.

3. Easy to Use

No-code tools are designed to be easy to use. You don't need any coding skills to create an app with these tools. Most no-code tools have a drag-and-drop interface, making it easy to create your app. This means you can focus on the functionality of your app rather than the technical details.

4. Customizable

No-code tools are highly customizable. You can create an app that meets your specific business needs. This means you don't have to settle for a one-size-fits-all solution. You can create an app that is tailored to your business requirements.

5. Scalable

No-code tools are also scalable. You can start with a small app and add more features as your business grows. This means your app can grow with your business, saving you the hassle of having to create a new app every time your business expands.

In summary, no-code tools offer many advantages for business owners who want to create their own apps. They are fast, cost-effective, easy to use, customizable, and scalable. If you want to create an app for your business, consider using a no-code tool. It will save you time and money, and help you get your app to market faster.

Popular no-code tools

No Code, No Problem: Creating Business Apps Without Coding Skills is the perfect guide for business owners who want to learn how to create their own business apps without the need for coding skills. In this subchapter, we will be discussing some of the most popular no-code tools that business owners can use to build their own apps.

1. Bubble

Bubble is a popular no-code tool that allows business owners to create web applications without any coding skills. It has an intuitive drag-and-drop interface that makes it easy to design and build custom web apps that can be used for a variety of purposes. Bubble also offers a wide range of templates and plugins that can be used to speed up the app development process.

2. Adalo

Adalo is another popular no-code tool that allows business owners to create mobile apps without the need for coding skills. It has a simple drag-and-drop interface that lets users design and build custom mobile apps that can be used for a variety of purposes. Adalo also offers a wide range of templates and plugins that can be used to speed up the app development process.

3. Glide

Glide is a no-code tool that allows business owners to create mobile apps from Google Sheets without any coding skills. It has a simple drag-and-drop interface that lets users design and build custom mobile apps that can be used for a variety of purposes. Glide also offers a wide range of templates and plugins that can be used to speed up the app development process.

4. Webflow

Webflow is a no-code tool that allows business owners to create responsive websites without any coding skills. It has a visual drag-and-drop interface that makes it easy to design and build custom websites that can be used for a variety of purposes. Webflow also offers a wide range of templates and plugins that can be used to speed up the website development process.

5. Zapier

Zapier is a no-code tool that allows business owners to automate workflows between different apps without any coding skills. It lets users create custom integrations between their favorite apps to automate repetitive tasks and save time. Zapier also offers a wide range of pre-built integrations that can be used to speed up the automation process.

In conclusion, these are some of the most popular no-code tools that business owners can use to create their own apps without the need for coding skills. With these tools, business owners can save time and money by building their own custom apps that can be used for a variety of purposes.

Demystifying no-code terminologies

Demystifying no-code terminologies

If you are a business owner looking to make an app for your business, you have probably heard the term "no-code" being thrown around a lot. However, if you are not from a technical background, you may find it challenging to understand some of the terminologies associated with no-code. In this subchapter, we will demystify some of the most common no-code terminologies.

1. Drag-and-drop: This is a term used to describe a visual interface that allows you to design your app by dragging and dropping elements onto a canvas. It is a core feature of many no-code platforms and enables users to create apps without having to write any code.

2. WYSIWYG: This stands for "what you see is what you get." It refers to the ability to see how your app will look and behave in real-time as you build it. This feature is also a core aspect of many no-code platforms and allows users to make changes to their app's design and functionality on the fly.

3. API: An API, or application programming interface, is a set of protocols, routines, and tools for building software applications. In the context of no-code, APIs are often used to integrate different software systems or services with your app. For example, you may use an API to integrate your app with a payment gateway or a social media platform.

4. Workflow: A workflow is a series of steps that define how a task or process is completed. In the context of no-code, workflows are often used to automate business processes. For example, you may use a workflow to automate your sales pipeline, where leads are automatically added to your CRM and then moved through a series of stages until they convert into customers.

5. Template: A template is a pre-built design or layout that you can use as a starting point for your app. Many no-code platforms offer a range of templates that can be customized to fit your specific needs.

By understanding these common no-code terminologies, you will be better equipped to navigate the world of no-code and build apps that are tailored to your business needs.

Planning Your Business App

Identifying your needs

Identifying Your Needs

Before you start creating an app for your business, it's important to identify your needs. This will help you determine what features your app should have and how it should function. Here are some things to consider when identifying your needs:

1. Purpose: What is the purpose of your app? Are you trying to increase sales, improve customer engagement, or streamline internal processes? Knowing the purpose of your app will help you determine what features and functions it should have.

2. Audience: Who is your target audience? Are you trying to reach existing customers, new customers, or both? Knowing your audience will help you determine what kind of user experience your app should provide.

3. Goals: What are your goals for the app? Are you trying to increase revenue, reduce costs, or improve efficiency? Knowing your goals will help you determine what kind of metrics you need to track and measure.

4. Content: What kind of content will your app provide? Will it be informational, interactive, or transactional? Knowing the type of content your app will provide will help you determine what kind of features and functions it should have.

5. Integration: What other systems or tools will your app need to integrate with? Will it need to integrate with your website, social media accounts, or other third-party tools? Knowing what integrations your app will need will help you determine what kind of APIs and services you need to use.

Once you have identified your needs, you can start selecting the right no-code tools and platforms to build your app. Remember, the key to success is to keep your app simple, user-friendly, and focused on solving a specific problem or meeting a specific need. By identifying your needs upfront, you can ensure that your app delivers value to your customers and helps you achieve your business goals.

Defining your goals

Defining Your Goals: The Importance of Knowing What You Want

As a business owner, you have a lot on your plate. You need to manage day-to-day operations, keep your customers happy, and stay on top of industry trends. With so much going on, it can be easy to lose sight of your long-term goals.

That's why it's crucial to take the time to define your goals. What do you want to achieve with your business? Where do you see it in five years? Ten years? Having a clear idea of your goals will help you make strategic decisions that move you closer to them.

When it comes to creating a business app, defining your goals is especially important. An app can be a powerful tool for growing your business, but only if it's aligned with your objectives. Here are some questions to ask yourself as you define your goals:

1. What problem do you want to solve?

Your app should be designed to solve a specific problem for your customers. What pain point are you trying to address? What frustrations do your customers have that your app can alleviate?

2. Who is your target audience?

Knowing your target audience is key to creating an app that resonates with them. Who are your ideal customers? What are their needs and preferences? How can your app address those needs in a way that's appealing to them?

3. What do you want your app to achieve?

What specific outcomes do you want your app to generate? Is it to increase customer engagement? Boost sales? Streamline operations? Having a clear idea of what you want to achieve will help you measure the success of your app and make adjustments as needed.

4. How will you measure success?

What metrics will you use to determine whether your app is achieving its goals? Will you track downloads, user engagement, or revenue generated? Knowing how you'll measure success will help you stay focused on your objectives and make data-driven decisions.

By taking the time to define your goals, you'll be better equipped to create an app that delivers value to your customers and drives growth for your business.

Identifying your target audience

Identifying Your Target Audience

One of the most important steps in creating a successful business app is identifying your target audience. Understanding who your app is for will help you tailor your app to their needs and preferences, making it more likely to be downloaded and used.

To start, consider the demographics of your ideal user. Are they young or old? Male or female? What is their income level and education level? These factors can help you determine the features and design elements that will appeal to your target audience.

You should also consider the needs and pain points of your target audience. What problems do they face in their daily lives that your app can solve? What features would make their lives easier or more enjoyable? By understanding these needs, you can create an app that truly resonates with your target audience.

Another key factor to consider is the platform on which your app will be used. Will it be a mobile app for iOS or Android devices? Or will it be a web app that can be accessed from any device with an internet connection? Knowing the platform your audience prefers will help you create an app that is accessible and user-friendly.

Finally, consider how your app can stand out from the competition. What unique features or benefits does it offer that other apps in your niche do not? By identifying your unique selling proposition, you can create an app that truly sets itself apart and appeals to your target audience.

In conclusion, identifying your target audience is a crucial step in creating a successful business app. By understanding the demographics, needs, and preferences of your ideal user, you can create an app that truly resonates with them and stands out from the competition. So take the time to do your research and get to know your target audience – it will pay off in the long run!

Researching your competition

As a business owner, it's important to research your competition to stay ahead of the game. Knowing what your competitors are doing can help you identify areas where you can improve and differentiate yourself from the competition. With no-code tools, researching your competition has become easier than ever before.

Start by identifying your competitors. This can be done by searching for businesses similar to yours on search engines and social media platforms. Make a list of the top competitors in your niche and start analyzing their websites, social media pages, and mobile apps (if they have any).

Look at their website design, user experience, and the features they offer. This can give you an idea of what your customers expect and where you can improve. If your competitors have mobile apps, download them and analyze their features, user interface, and user experience. This can help you identify gaps in their offering that you can fill with your own app.

Another way to research your competition is by analyzing their social media pages. Look at their followers, engagement rates, and the content they post. This can help you identify what kind of content resonates with your target audience and what doesn't.

Once you have identified your competition and analyzed their online presence, it's time to identify what sets you apart. Use the information you have gathered to create a unique value proposition for your business. This can be done by identifying gaps in your competitor's offering and filling them with your own app.

No-code tools make it easy to create a mobile app that meets the unique needs of your business. With no coding skills required, you can create an app that stands out from the competition and provides value to your customers.

In conclusion, researching your competition is essential for any business owner looking to stay ahead of the game. With no-code tools, this task has become easier than ever before. By analyzing your competitor's online presence and identifying gaps in their offering, you can create a unique value proposition for your business and create a mobile app that meets the unique needs of your customers.

Defining your app features

Defining Your App Features

When it comes to creating an app for your business, it can be easy to get lost in the excitement of all the possibilities. However, before you jump into building your app, it's important to define the features that will make it unique and valuable to your target audience.

To start, consider the needs and pain points of your customers. What problems are they looking to solve? What features would make their lives easier or more enjoyable? By focusing on their needs, you can create an app that is tailored to their specific interests and preferences.

Once you've identified the core features that will make your app stand out, it's important to prioritize them. This means deciding which features are essential to the functionality of your app and which are nice-to-haves. By prioritizing your features, you can ensure that you are focusing on the elements that will have the biggest impact on your users.

Another important consideration is the user experience (UX) of your app. This includes the design, layout, and ease of use of your app. To create a great UX, it's important to keep your app simple and intuitive. This means avoiding cluttered screens and confusing navigation. By making your app easy to use, you can increase user engagement and retention.

Finally, it's important to consider the technical requirements of your app. This includes the platform you will be building on, the programming language you will be using, and any third-party integrations that may be necessary. By understanding the technical requirements of your app, you can ensure that you have the necessary resources and skills to build it successfully.

In conclusion, defining your app features is an essential part of creating a successful business app. By focusing on the needs of your customers, prioritizing your features, creating a great UX, and understanding the technical requirements, you can build an app that is tailored to your audience and drives business growth.

Designing Your Business App

Choosing the right design tools

Choosing the right design tools is an essential part of creating business apps without coding skills. With so many different options out there, it can be overwhelming trying to figure out which tools are the best fit for your specific needs.

One of the first things to consider is the type of app you are looking to create. Are you building a mobile app, a web app, or both? This will help you determine which design tools are most appropriate for your project.

For mobile apps, there are several popular design tools available, including Sketch, Adobe XD, and Figma. These tools allow you to create high-fidelity designs for iOS and Android devices, and they offer a range of features such as vector editing, prototyping, and collaboration.

If you are building a web app, you may want to consider using design tools such as Webflow, Bubble, or Wix. These tools allow you to design and build your web app without any coding skills, and they offer a range of features such as responsive design, drag-and-drop builders, and integrations with popular services like Stripe and Zapier.

Another important factor to consider when choosing design tools is your budget. Some tools, like Sketch and Adobe XD, require a monthly subscription fee, while others, like Figma and Canva, offer free or low-cost options. It's important to weigh the features and benefits of each tool against the cost to determine which option is right for you.

Finally, it's important to consider the learning curve of each design tool. Some tools may be more intuitive and user-friendly, while others may require more time and effort to master. Consider your own level of experience with design tools, as well as the experience of your team members who will be working on the project.

In conclusion, choosing the right design tools is an important part of creating business apps without coding skills. By considering factors such as the type of app you are building, your budget, and the learning curve of each tool, you can select the best option for your specific needs and create a high-quality, professional-looking app that meets the needs of your business.

Creating wireframes

Creating wireframes is an essential step towards building a successful app for your business. A wireframe is a visual representation of your app's layout and structure, providing a roadmap for the development process. Wireframes serve as the foundation for the design and development of your app, ensuring that your team is aligned and working towards a common goal.

In this chapter, we will discuss the process of creating wireframes, the tools you can use, and best practices to ensure that your wireframes are effective in communicating your app's design and functionality.

The first step in creating wireframes is to define your app's purpose and target audience. Understanding your app's purpose and target audience will help you create a wireframe that meets your business goals and resonates with your target users. You should consider your app's features, functionalities, and user experience when creating wireframes.

Once you have a clear understanding of your app's purpose and target audience, you can start sketching your wireframes. Sketching is a low-fidelity way of creating wireframes, allowing you to quickly iterate and refine your ideas. You can use a pen and paper or a digital sketching tool to create your wireframes.

The next step is to create digital wireframes using a wireframing tool. There are several wireframing tools available, such as Figma, Sketch, and Adobe XD, that you can use to create your wireframes. These tools offer pre-built templates, libraries of UI elements, and drag-and-drop functionality, making it easy to create wireframes.

When creating wireframes, it's important to keep in mind the user experience. Your wireframes should be easy to understand, navigate, and interact with. You should also pay attention to the layout, typography, and color scheme to ensure that your wireframes are visually appealing and consistent with your brand.

In conclusion, wireframes are an essential step towards building a successful app for your business. They provide a visual representation of your app's layout and structure, ensuring that your team is aligned and working towards a common goal. When creating wireframes, it's important to define your app's purpose and target audience, sketch your ideas, and use digital wireframing tools to create your wireframes. By following these best practices, you can create effective wireframes that communicate your app's design and functionality.

Designing the user interface

Designing the user interface is a crucial step when creating an app for your business. A well-designed user interface can make all the difference in how users perceive and interact with your app. In this subchapter, we will explore some key principles and best practices for designing a user-friendly interface using no-code tools.

First and foremost, it's essential to understand your target audience and their needs. What are they looking for in your app, and what features are most important to them? Once you have a good understanding of your users, you can start to design a user interface that meets their needs and expectations.

One of the most important elements of a user interface is its layout. You want to make sure that your app's layout is intuitive and easy to navigate. Use clear and concise labels for buttons and menu items, and group related features together. Avoid cluttering the interface with too many elements, as this can overwhelm users and make it difficult for them to find what they're looking for.

When it comes to colors, choose a palette that is consistent with your brand's colors and is easy on the eyes. Use contrasting colors to make important elements stand out, such as buttons or calls to action. Be mindful of colorblind users and ensure that your app is accessible to all.

Typography is another important element of a user interface. Choose a font that is easy to read on different screen sizes and resolutions. Use font size and weight to create hierarchy and emphasize important information.

Finally, consider the overall user experience when designing your interface. Make sure that your app is responsive and works well on different devices and platforms. Test your app with real users to get feedback on how to improve the interface and make it more user-friendly.

In conclusion, designing a user interface for your business app is a critical step in creating a successful product. By following these principles and best practices, you can create an interface that is intuitive, easy to use, and meets the needs of your target audience. With no-code tools, you don't need to be a designer or developer to create a great user interface for your app.

Creating a brand identity

Creating a brand identity is essential for any business, regardless of its size or industry. A brand identity refers to the visual and emotional characteristics that distinguish your business from others. It is a way to communicate your values, personality, and mission to your target audience.

When creating a brand identity for your business app, there are a few key elements to consider. These include your logo, color scheme, typography, and overall design aesthetic.

Your logo is the centerpiece of your brand identity. It should be simple, memorable, and reflective of your brand's values and personality. If you don't have design skills, there are plenty of no-code tools that can help you create a professional-looking logo in minutes.

Your color scheme should be consistent across all aspects of your brand identity, from your logo to your app's user interface. Choose colors that evoke the emotions you want your audience to feel when they interact with your brand.

Typography is another important aspect of brand identity. Choose fonts that are easy to read and reflect your brand's personality. If you're not sure where to start, there are plenty of no-code tools that offer pre-made font pairings.

Finally, your overall design aesthetic should be consistent with your brand's personality and values. Whether you opt for a minimalist, modern design or a more traditional look, make sure it aligns with your brand's messaging.

Creating a strong brand identity is not just about aesthetics. It is also about building a connection with your audience. By creating a brand identity that reflects your values and personality, you can establish trust with your customers and differentiate yourself from your competitors.

In conclusion, creating a brand identity is a crucial step in developing a successful business app. By paying attention to your logo, color scheme, typography, and overall design aesthetic, you can create a brand identity that resonates with your target audience and sets your business apart from the competition. With no-code tools, it's easier than ever to create a professional-looking brand identity for your business app without any coding skills.

Building Your Business App

Choosing the right no-code platform

Choosing the right no-code platform can be overwhelming, especially if you're new to the concept of creating business apps without coding skills. With so many options available, how do you know which one is right for you?

Firstly, you need to consider your business needs. What kind of app do you want to create? Is it a mobile app or a web app? What features do you need? Will you need to integrate with other systems or services? Answering these questions will help you narrow down your options.

Next, you should consider the ease of use and user interface of the no-code platform. You want a platform that is intuitive and easy to navigate, so you don't waste time trying to figure out how to use it. Look for platforms that offer drag-and-drop functionality and pre-built templates to make your app development process faster and more efficient.

It's also important to consider the level of customization offered by the no-code platform. You want a platform that allows you to customize your app to your unique business needs. Look for platforms that offer a variety of design tools, options for adding custom code, and integrations with other services.

Another important factor to consider is the support and resources offered by the no-code platform. Look for platforms that offer a robust knowledge base, tutorials, and customer support to help you troubleshoot any issues you may encounter.

Finally, you should consider the pricing model of the no-code platform. Look for platforms that offer flexible pricing options, such as pay-as-you-go or monthly subscriptions, to ensure that you're not paying for features you don't need.

In summary, choosing the right no-code platform requires careful consideration of your business needs, ease of use, customization, support and resources, and pricing model. By taking the time to evaluate these factors, you can select a platform that will help you create a business app without coding skills, quickly and efficiently.

Building your app structure

Building Your App Structure

When it comes to building a successful business app, structure is key. The structure of your app will determine its functionality, user experience, and overall success. In this chapter, we'll explore the steps you need to take to build a solid app structure that will help you achieve your business goals.

1. Identify your app's purpose and goals

Before you start building your app, you need to identify its purpose and goals. What problem does your app solve? Who is your target audience? What features does your app need to have to meet your business goals? Answering these questions will help you determine what kind of app structure you need to build.

2. Create a wireframe

A wireframe is a visual representation of your app's layout and functionality. It's like a blueprint for your app. Creating a wireframe will help you visualize the app structure and make any necessary changes before you start building. There are many tools available that can help you create a wireframe, such as Figma, Sketch, or Adobe XD.

3. Choose your app's navigation style

Navigation is an important aspect of your app's structure. It allows users to move through your app and access its features. There are several navigation styles to choose from, such as tab bar navigation, hamburger menu navigation, or bottom navigation. Choose the navigation style that best suits your app's purpose and goals.

4. Organize your app's content

Content organization is another important aspect of your app's structure. You need to consider how you will organize your app's content to make it easy for users to find what they're looking for. This can be done through categories, tags, filters, or search functionalities. Make sure your app's content is easy to navigate and find.

5. Test and iterate

Once you've built your app structure, it's important to test it and iterate as necessary. You can use user testing or analytics tools to gather feedback on your app's structure and make any necessary changes. Testing and iterating will help you create an app structure that meets your business goals and provides a great user experience.

In conclusion, building a solid app structure is essential for creating a successful business app. By following these steps, you can create an app structure that meets your business goals and provides a great user experience. Remember to identify your app's purpose and goals, create a wireframe, choose your app's navigation style, organize your app's content, and test and iterate as necessary. With these steps, you'll be well on your way to creating a great business app without coding skills.

Integrating app features

Integrating app features is crucial to creating a successful business app without coding skills. No matter the purpose of the app, integrating features such as user authentication, data storage, and push notifications can greatly enhance the user experience and increase engagement, ultimately leading to increased revenue and growth for your business.

One of the easiest ways to integrate features into your app without coding is by using third-party services like Zapier, Integromat, or Bubble. These platforms offer pre-built integrations with popular services like Google Sheets, Mailchimp, and Slack, allowing you to easily connect your app to these services and automate tasks. For example, if you have an e-commerce app, you can integrate with Stripe to process payments, or with Shipstation to manage shipping and tracking.

Another way to integrate features into your app is by using no-code tools like Glide or Adalo. These platforms allow you to create custom features for your app using pre-built templates and drag-and-drop interfaces. For instance, you can use Adalo to create a user authentication system, data storage, and push notifications in just a few clicks.

It's essential to understand the purpose of your app and the features that will provide the most value to your users. For instance, if you're creating a fitness app, integrating features like workout tracking, progress tracking, and a community forum can enhance the user experience and increase engagement. Similarly, if you're creating an e-commerce app, integrating features like product search, shopping cart, and wish list can enhance the user experience and increase sales.

In conclusion, integrating app features is an essential aspect of creating a successful business app without coding. By using third-party services, no-code tools, and understanding the purpose of your app, you can create custom features that will enhance the user experience, increase engagement, and drive growth for your business.

Adding content to your app

Adding Content to Your App

Once you've designed the layout and functionality of your app, it's time to start adding content. This is where you can really make your app stand out and provide value to your users. Here are some tips for adding content to your app:

1. Know your audience: Before you start creating content, make sure you understand your target audience. What are their interests and pain points? What kind of content are they looking for? This will help you create relevant and engaging content that will keep them coming back to your app.

2. Create a content plan: Just like with any other marketing strategy, it's important to have a plan for your app content. This will help you stay organized and consistent with your updates. Your plan should include the types of content you'll create, how often you'll post, and who will be responsible for creating and publishing the content.

3. Use a variety of content types: Don't just stick to one type of content in your app. Mix it up with videos, images, infographics, and written content. This will keep your users engaged and interested in what you have to offer.

4. Keep it simple: When it comes to content in your app, less is often more. Keep your content simple and to the point, and make sure it's easy to read and understand. Use clear headlines and bullet points to break up longer pieces of text.

5. Test and measure: Once you start adding content to your app, it's important to track its performance. Use analytics tools to see which types of content are resonating with your users and which ones aren't. This will help you make adjustments to your content plan and ensure that you're providing the best possible experience for your users.

Adding content to your app is an ongoing process that requires time and effort. But by following these tips, you can create a content strategy that will help you engage your users and provide value to your business.

Testing your app

Testing Your App

Once you have created your business app using no-code tools, it is important to test it thoroughly before launching it to the public. Testing your app can help you identify any bugs or glitches that may affect user experience and your app's performance. In this section, we will explore some of the best practices for testing your app.

1. Test Early and Often

Testing your app should be an ongoing process that begins as soon as you start developing it. You should test your app at every stage of development to ensure that it works as expected. This will help you catch any errors or issues early on, which will save you time and money in the long run.

2. Use Real-World Scenarios

When testing your app, it is important to use real-world scenarios to simulate how users will interact with it. This will help you identify any design flaws or usability issues that may affect user experience. For example, you could ask your friends or family to try out your app and provide feedback on their experience.

3. Test Across Multiple Devices

Make sure to test your app across multiple devices and platforms to ensure that it works seamlessly on all of them. This includes testing on different versions of iOS and Android, as well as different screen sizes and resolutions. This will help you identify any compatibility issues that may affect user experience.

4. Use Automated Testing Tools

There are many automated testing tools available that can help you test your app more efficiently. These tools can simulate user interactions and provide detailed reports on any errors or issues that are found. Some popular automated testing tools include Appium, Calabash, and Selenium.

5. Get Feedback from Users

Finally, it is important to get feedback from users once your app is launched. This will help you identify any issues that may have been missed during the testing process and provide valuable insights into how users are interacting with your app. You can use tools like App Store reviews, surveys, and focus groups to gather feedback from users.

In summary, testing your app is a crucial step in the app development process. By testing early and often, using real-world scenarios, testing across multiple devices, using automated testing tools, and getting feedback from users, you can ensure that your app is functioning as expected and providing a great user experience.

Launching Your Business App

Pre-launch checklist

A pre-launch checklist is an essential part of any app development process, whether you are creating a business app with no coding skills or not. It helps you ensure that your app is fully functional and ready for launch. Here are some important items that should be on your pre-launch checklist.

1. User Testing - Before the launch of your app, you need to ensure that it has been tested thoroughly by users. Reach out to beta testers and gather feedback on the user experience, functionality, and potential bugs. Make sure you have taken actions based on the feedback before launching.

2. App Store Optimization (ASO) - ASO is the process of optimizing your app to rank higher in app store search results. Make sure that your app's title, description, and keywords are optimized for search engines.

3. Marketing Materials - Make sure that you have all the necessary marketing materials ready for the launch of your app. This includes screenshots, demo videos, and a press release. You need to create a buzz around your app before launching it so that it has a better chance of being successful.

4. App Security - Security is a critical aspect of app development. Make sure that your app is secure and has been tested for vulnerabilities. Security breaches can cause significant damage to your business reputation and lead to legal issues.

5. App Analytics - You need to have a system in place to track your app's performance. This includes monitoring user engagement, retention, and revenue. This information can help you make data-driven decisions and improve your app.

6. App Updates - You should have a plan in place for future updates to your app. This includes bug fixes, feature updates, and new releases. Your app should be continuously updated to ensure that it remains relevant and competitive.

In conclusion, a pre-launch checklist is an essential part of app development. It ensures that your app is functional, secure, and optimized for success. Make sure that you have all the necessary items on your checklist before launching your app.

Launching your app on app stores

Launching Your App on App Stores

Once you have designed and developed your app using no-code tools, the next step is to launch it on app stores. This step is crucial because it is how your potential customers will find and download your app. In this subchapter, we will discuss the process of launching your app on app stores.

Before launching your app, you need to make sure that it is ready for the market. This means that you need to test your app thoroughly to ensure that it is bug-free and works smoothly on different devices. You should also make sure that the app meets the guidelines and policies of the app store you are targeting.

The two most popular app stores are the Apple App Store and the Google Play Store. Here are the steps to launch your app on these stores:

Apple App Store:

1. Create an Apple Developer account and sign in to App Store Connect.
2. Create a new app and fill in the required information, including the app name, description, keywords, and pricing.
3. Upload screenshots and videos of your app.
4. Submit your app for review.

Once your app is approved, it will be available on the App Store for users to download.

Google Play Store:

1. Create a Google Play Developer account and sign in to the Google Play Console.
2. Create a new app and fill in the required information, including the app name, description, keywords, and pricing.
3. Upload screenshots and videos of your app.
4. Submit your app for review.

Once your app is approved, it will be available on the Google Play Store for users to download.

In addition to the Apple App Store and Google Play Store, there are other app stores that you can consider, such as the Amazon Appstore and the Samsung Galaxy Store.

Launching your app on app stores is just the first step. You also need to promote your app to reach your target audience. You can use social media, email marketing, and paid advertising to promote your app. You should also ask your customers for feedback and continuously improve your app based on their feedback.

In summary, launching your app on app stores is an important step in making your app available to your target audience. Make sure that your app is ready for the market, meets the guidelines and policies of the app store, and promote it to reach your target audience.

Marketing your app

Marketing Your App

Creating a business app is just the first step in your journey towards achieving your business goals. The next step is to ensure that the app gets the right visibility and reaches the right audience. This is where marketing your app comes in.

Marketing your app is crucial to its success. It is the process of creating awareness about your app, building its reputation, and promoting it to your target audience. Here are some tips to help you market your app successfully.

1. Define your target audience

Before you start marketing your app, you need to know who your target audience is. Your target audience is the group of people who are most likely to download and use your app. It could be a specific age group, location, or interest group. Once you have defined your target audience, you can tailor your marketing efforts to reach them effectively.

2. Create a compelling app description

Your app description is the first thing that potential users will see when they come across your app on the app store. It needs to be compelling enough to convince them to download and use your app. Your app description should clearly state what your app does, its features and benefits, and how it can help your users.

3. Use social media to promote your app

Social media is a powerful tool for marketing your app. You can use social media platforms like Facebook, Twitter, and Instagram to promote your app to your target audience. You can also use social media ads to reach a larger audience.

4. Leverage app store optimization (ASO)

App store optimization (ASO) is the process of optimizing your app to rank higher in the app store search results. It involves using relevant keywords, optimizing your app name and description, and getting positive reviews and ratings. ASO can help increase your app visibility and downloads.

5. Offer incentives and promotions

Offering incentives and promotions is a great way to encourage users to download and use your app. You can offer free trials, discounts, or exclusive content to users who download your app. This can help increase your app downloads and user engagement.

In conclusion, marketing your app is crucial to its success. By defining your target audience, creating a compelling app description, using social media to promote your app, leveraging app store optimization, and offering incentives and promotions, you can effectively market your app and achieve your business goals.

Measuring your app's success

Measuring your app's success

Creating a business app without coding is no small feat. It requires time, effort, and resources. But how do you measure the success of your app? The answer to this question is crucial, as it allows you to determine if your app is meeting your business goals.

The first step in measuring your app's success is to identify your business objectives. What do you want your app to achieve? Is it to increase sales, improve customer engagement, or streamline operations? Once you have identified your objectives, you can then set specific, measurable, achievable, relevant, and time-bound goals (SMART goals) that align with your business objectives.

One of the most important metrics to measure the success of your app is user engagement. This metric tells you how many people are using your app, how often they are using it, and how long they are spending on your app. User engagement can be measured through various metrics such as daily active users (DAU), monthly active users (MAU), retention rate, and session length.

Another critical metric to measure is the conversion rate. This metric tells you how many people are taking the desired action on your app, such as making a purchase or filling out a form. You can track the conversion rate by setting up conversion tracking in your app analytics.

Customer satisfaction is also an essential metric to measure. You can gather feedback from your customers through surveys or in-app feedback forms. This feedback will help you understand what your customers like and dislike about your app, and you can use this information to make improvements.

Finally, you should also measure your app's return on investment (ROI). This metric tells you how much revenue your app is generating compared to the cost of developing and maintaining it. To calculate the ROI, you need to track the revenue generated by your app and subtract the costs of development and maintenance.

In conclusion, measuring your app's success requires a combination of metrics that align with your business objectives. By tracking these metrics regularly, you can make data-driven decisions and improve your app's performance. Remember, the success of your app is not only about the number of downloads but also about how well it helps you achieve your business goals.

Enhancing Your Business App

Analyzing user feedback

Analyzing user feedback is a crucial step in the process of creating a successful business app. It allows you to identify what works and what doesn't work for your users, which in turn helps you make informed decisions about how to improve your app.

There are several ways to gather user feedback, including surveys, user testing, and analytics. Surveys can be conducted through email, in-app pop-ups, or social media, and provide valuable information about user preferences and satisfaction. User testing involves observing users as they interact with your app and asking for their feedback in real-time. Analytics tools, such as Google Analytics, can provide detailed data on user behavior and engagement within your app.

Once you have gathered user feedback, it's important to analyze it in a systematic and objective way. Look for patterns and trends in the data, such as common complaints or areas where users are spending the most time. Use this information to identify areas for improvement and prioritize your development efforts accordingly.

It's also important to keep in mind that not all user feedback is created equal. Some users may have specific preferences or needs that do not necessarily reflect the opinions of the majority. It's important to weigh feedback from a variety of sources and take a holistic approach to decision-making.

Ultimately, analyzing user feedback should be an ongoing process throughout the development and maintenance of your app. Regularly gathering and analyzing feedback can help you stay ahead of the curve and ensure that your app is meeting the needs of your users.

Improving user experience

Improving User Experience

As a business owner, creating an app for your business is one thing, but ensuring that the app provides a great user experience is another. User experience is essential in determining the success of your app, and it is crucial to keep it in mind throughout the development process.

Here are some tips to help you improve user experience in your business app:

1. Keep it simple

Users prefer apps that are easy to use and navigate. Avoid cluttering your app with too many features or confusing menus. Keep it simple and intuitive, and your users will appreciate it.

2. Focus on speed

Slow loading times can be frustrating for users, and they may abandon your app if it takes too long to load. Optimize your app's performance to ensure that it loads quickly and runs smoothly.

3. Use clear and concise language

Your app's copy should be easy to read and understand. Use clear and concise language to communicate your message, and avoid technical jargon that may confuse your users.

4. Make it visually appealing

The design of your app is just as important as its functionality. Use appealing colors, fonts, and graphics to make your app visually appealing and engaging.

5. Test and iterate

Once you have launched your app, it's essential to test it thoroughly and gather feedback from users. Use this feedback to iterate and make improvements to your app to provide a better user experience.

By following these tips, you can create a business app that not only serves its purpose but also provides a great user experience. Remember, happy users are more likely to recommend your app, which can lead to more business and increased revenue.

Adding new features to your app

As a business owner, you may be looking to add new features to your app to improve the user experience and increase engagement. The good news is that with no-code tools, adding new features to your app has never been easier.

One way to add new features to your app is by using pre-built integrations. Many no-code platforms offer integrations with popular tools like Google Analytics, Stripe, and Zapier. By integrating these tools into your app, you can add features like payment processing, tracking user data, and automating tasks.

Another way to add new features to your app is by using third-party plugins. Many no-code platforms have marketplaces where you can browse and install plugins created by other users. These plugins can add a wide variety of features to your app, from social media sharing buttons to chatbots.

If you can't find the exact feature you're looking for in a pre-built integration or plugin, you can always create it yourself using no-code tools. Many no-code platforms offer drag-and-drop interfaces that make it easy to create custom features without writing a single line of code.

For example, let's say you want to add a feature that allows users to schedule appointments with your business directly through your app. With a no-code tool like Bubble, you could create a custom form that collects user information and syncs with your Google Calendar to automatically schedule appointments.

When adding new features to your app, it's important to keep the user experience in mind. Make sure the new feature fits seamlessly into your app's design and doesn't disrupt the user flow. You should also test any new features thoroughly to ensure they work properly and don't introduce any bugs.

In conclusion, adding new features to your app is a great way to improve the user experience and increase engagement. With no-code tools, adding new features has never been easier, whether you're using pre-built integrations, third-party plugins, or creating custom features yourself. Just remember to keep the user experience in mind and test any new features thoroughly before launching.

Maintaining your app

Maintaining Your App

Once you have created and launched your business app, it is important to maintain it to ensure that it stays up-to-date, secure, and relevant to your users. Here are some tips on how to maintain your app:

1. Regular updates

The first step to maintaining your app is to regularly update it with new features, bug fixes, and security patches. This will keep your app running smoothly and ensure that your users have the best possible experience.

2. User feedback

Listen to your users and take their feedback into consideration when making updates to your app. This will help you improve the user experience and keep your users engaged with your app.

3. Analytics

Track your app's performance through analytics to identify areas that need improvement or opportunities for growth. This will help you make data-driven decisions about how to improve your app and increase engagement with your users.

4. Security

Make sure that your app is secure by regularly testing and updating security measures. This will help protect your users' personal information and prevent any potential data breaches.

5. Compatibility

Stay up-to-date with new technology and ensure that your app is compatible with the latest devices and operating systems. This will help you reach a wider audience and ensure that your app remains relevant in a constantly evolving digital landscape.

By following these tips, you can maintain your app and ensure that it remains a valuable asset to your business. Remember, an app is never truly finished – it requires ongoing maintenance and updates to stay relevant and engaging to your users.

Conclusion

Recap of the book's key points

Recap of the book's key points

No Code, No Problem: Creating Business Apps Without Coding Skills is a comprehensive guide for business owners who want to create their own apps without any coding skills. Throughout the book, the author has explained the importance of no-code tools and how they can help businesses save time and money. In this subchapter, we will recap the key points of the book that every business owner should keep in mind when creating an app.

1. The Power of No-Code Tools

No-code tools are designed to help people create apps without any coding skills. They provide a user-friendly interface that allows anyone to create an app by simply dragging and dropping elements. These tools have revolutionized the app development industry and have made it possible for businesses to create apps quickly and easily.

2. Understanding Your Business Needs

Before you start creating your app, it's important to understand your business needs. You need to identify the problem you want to solve and the audience you want to target. Understanding your business needs will help you create an app that meets your requirements and satisfies your customers.

3. Choosing the Right No-Code Tool

There are many no-code tools available in the market, and it's important to choose the right one for your business. You should consider factors such as ease of use, functionality, and pricing when selecting a tool. It's also essential to choose a tool that offers the features you need to create your app.

4. Designing Your App

Designing your app is a crucial step in the app development process. You need to create a user-friendly interface that is easy to navigate and visually appealing. You should also ensure that your app meets the design guidelines of the platform you're creating it for.

5. Testing and Launching Your App

Once you've designed your app, it's important to test it thoroughly before launching it. You should test your app on different devices and platforms to ensure that it works correctly. After testing, you can launch your app on the platform of your choice.

In conclusion, the book No Code, No Problem: Creating Business Apps Without Coding Skills provides valuable insights and tips for businesses that want to create their own apps without any coding skills. By understanding the power of no-code tools, identifying your business needs, choosing the right no-code tool, designing your app, and testing and launching your app, you can create an app that meets your requirements and satisfies your customers.

Final thoughts on no-code app development

Final Thoughts on No-Code App Development

No-code app development has become an essential tool for businesses looking to create custom apps quickly and efficiently. Whether you are a business owner looking to develop an app for your company or an entrepreneur looking to create a new app for your customers, no-code app development can help you achieve your goals without requiring any coding skills.

One of the primary benefits of no-code app development is that it allows businesses to focus on their core competencies. Instead of spending time and resources on learning how to code or hiring expensive developers, businesses can use no-code app development platforms to create apps that meet their specific needs. This approach allows businesses to streamline their operations, reduce costs, and increase efficiency.

Another significant advantage of no-code app development is its flexibility. No-code app development platforms offer a wide range of customization options, allowing businesses to create apps that are tailored to their specific needs. Whether it's creating a custom interface, integrating with third-party services, or adding new features, businesses can easily modify their apps to meet their evolving needs.

Finally, no-code app development is incredibly user-friendly. Most no-code app development platforms offer intuitive interfaces that are easy to use, even for those with no coding experience. This means that businesses can create apps quickly and easily, without the need for extensive training or technical expertise.

In conclusion, no-code app development is a game-changer for businesses looking to create custom apps quickly, efficiently, and cost-effectively. Whether you're a small business owner looking to develop an app to streamline your operations or an entrepreneur looking to create a new app for your customers, no-code app development platforms can help you achieve your goals without requiring any coding skills. So why wait? Start exploring the world of no-code app development today and discover how it can transform your business.

Future of no-code app development

The future of no-code app development is incredibly bright, and it's only getting brighter. With the rise of platforms like Bubble, Adalo, and Glide, creating powerful, enterprise-grade apps is easier than ever before. And as these platforms continue to mature and expand, the possibilities for what you can do with no-code will only become more impressive.

One of the most exciting things about the future of no-code app development is that it's becoming more accessible to non-technical users. In the past, creating an app required a deep understanding of coding languages like JavaScript and Python. But with no-code platforms, you can build an app using simple drag-and-drop interfaces and visual editors. This means that anyone can create an app, regardless of their technical background.

Another trend in the future of no-code app development is the rise of AI and machine learning. As these technologies become more advanced and accessible, they will enable even more powerful and sophisticated apps to be developed without any coding skills. For example, you could use AI to automatically generate content for your app or to analyze user data and make personalized recommendations.

No-code app development is also becoming more collaborative. Platforms like Bubble allow multiple users to work on the same app simultaneously, making it easier for teams to collaborate on app development projects. This means that businesses can bring together designers, marketers, and other stakeholders to work on an app project without needing to hire a dedicated development team.

Finally, the future of no-code app development is all about integration. As more and more businesses rely on multiple software tools to run their operations, no-code platforms are making it easier to integrate these tools into a single app. This means that you can create a custom app that connects with all of your existing tools, streamlining your workflow and making your business more efficient.

In conclusion, the future of no-code app development is incredibly exciting. As these platforms continue to evolve, they will enable businesses of all sizes to create powerful, sophisticated apps without needing any coding skills. Whether you're looking to streamline your workflow, improve your customer experience, or create a new revenue stream, no-code app development is the key to unlocking your business's full potential.

Call to action

As a business owner, your ultimate goal is to increase your revenue and make your business successful. One way to achieve this is by creating a mobile app for your business. However, if you are not tech-savvy, the thought of developing an app might seem daunting. But with the advent of no-code app development platforms, creating an app for your business has never been easier.

No-code app development platforms are designed to help individuals with no coding skills create fully-functional mobile apps. These platforms come with pre-built templates, drag-and-drop tools, and easy-to-use features that make app development a breeze. With no-code app development, you can develop an app for your business in a matter of hours or days, depending on the complexity of your project.

The benefits of creating an app for your business are numerous. For one, it helps you reach a wider audience and connect with your customers more effectively. An app can also help you retain customers by providing them with a seamless experience and keeping them engaged with your brand. Additionally, an app can increase your revenue by providing you with new revenue streams, such as in-app purchases or advertising.

So, if you are a business owner looking to create an app for your business, the time to act is now. With no-code app development platforms, you can create an app that meets your business needs and goals. Start by researching different no-code app development platforms and choose one that best suits your needs. Then, map out your app's features, design, and functionality, and start building. Remember to test your app thoroughly before launching it to ensure that it is bug-free and user-friendly.

In conclusion, creating an app for your business using no-code app development platforms is a game-changer for business owners without coding skills. It is an excellent way to reach a wider audience, retain customers, and increase your revenue. So, take the first step today and start creating an app that will take your business to the next level.

Bonus Chapter: Case Studies

Real-life examples of successful no-code business apps

Real-life examples of successful no-code business apps

No-code app development is gaining popularity among business owners who want to create their own apps without the need for coding skills. With the advancement of technology and the availability of no-code app development platforms, creating a business app has become easier than ever.

Here are some real-life examples of successful no-code business apps that have been created by business owners using no-code app development tools:

1. Trello - Trello is a project management app that allows teams to collaborate and manage projects in real-time. It was created using no-code app development tools like Bubble and Zapier.

2. Groupon - Groupon is a deals and coupons app that offers discounts on products and services. It was created using no-code app development tools like WordPress and WooCommerce.

3. Basecamp - Basecamp is a project management and team communication app that helps teams stay organized and productive. It was created using no-code app development tools like Ruby on Rails and Heroku.

4. Mailchimp - Mailchimp is a marketing automation and email marketing app that helps businesses grow their email list and send targeted campaigns. It was created using no-code app development tools like WordPress and Zapier.

5. Buffer - Buffer is a social media management app that helps businesses schedule and publish content on different social media platforms. It was created using no-code app development tools like Ruby on Rails and Heroku.

These successful no-code business apps are proof that you don't need coding skills to create a successful business app. With the right no-code app development platform and tools, you can turn your app idea into a reality and grow your business.

Lessons learned from each case study

Lessons learned from each case study

In each of the case studies presented in this book, there are valuable lessons that business owners can learn from. These lessons can help guide you in developing your own business app using no-code platforms.

Lesson 1: Identify your business needs

The first lesson to be learned from our case studies is the importance of identifying your business needs. Before creating an app, you need to determine what your business needs are and how an app can help you achieve them. This will help you create a more focused and effective app that addresses your specific business requirements.

Lesson 2: Choose the right no-code platform

Another lesson we learned from our case studies is the importance of choosing the right no-code platform. There are many no-code platforms available, each with its own strengths and weaknesses. It is important to choose a platform that can provide the features and functions that your app needs.

Lesson 3: Plan and design your app carefully

Planning and designing your app carefully is crucial to its success. In our case studies, we saw how careful planning and design can lead to a more user-friendly and effective app. This includes designing an intuitive user interface, creating a logical navigation structure, and ensuring that the app is visually appealing.

Lesson 4: Test and iterate your app

Testing and iterating your app is also important to its success. In our case studies, we saw how testing and iterating helped improve the functionality and usability of the app. This involves testing the app with real users, soliciting feedback, and making necessary improvements based on that feedback.

Lesson 5: Focus on user experience

Finally, a key lesson we learned from our case studies is the importance of focusing on user experience. A good app should be easy to use, intuitive, and visually appealing. This requires a deep understanding of your target audience and their needs, as well as a commitment to ongoing improvement.

By learning from these case studies, business owners can create their own successful no-code apps that meet their specific business needs and provide value to their customers.